short o

nds & Letters 4

KNOWLEDGE BOOKS

hop	mop
shop	cot
dot	rod
sock	

O

hop

mop

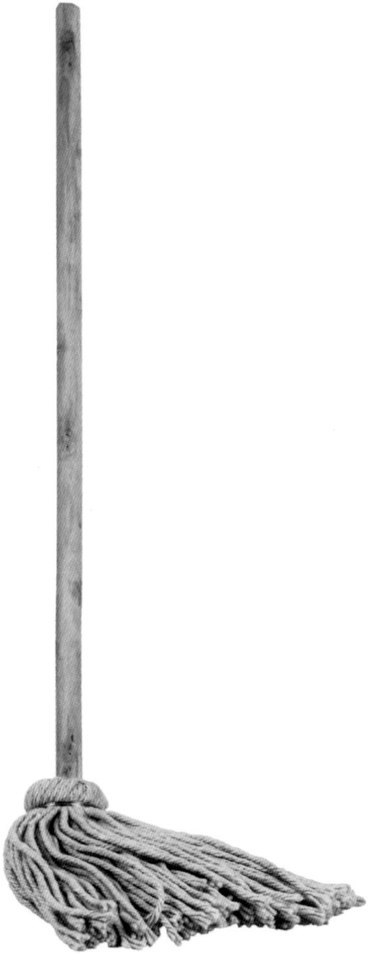

shop

Save the Children
Australia
Save the Children
Australia
Op Shop
SHOP HERE AND
CREATE BETTER
FOR CHILDRE
Save the Children
Thanks for your support
CLOSED

cot

dot

rod

sock

hop	mop
shop	cot
dot	rod
sock	